"I didn't Do It!"

By Sherrie Weaver

Cover Design by Design Dynamics

Typography by MarketForce

Publishing by Great Quotations Publishing Co.,
Glendale Heights, IL

Library of Congress Catalog Card number: 97-77638

ISBN 1-56245-333-5

Printed in U.S.A.

This book is dedicated to Jessica and Seth, who have used most of the really good excuses at one time or another. To Harley & Mike, who have heard most of them, from me. And to my brother, who is pretty sure everything is still my fault.

Introduction

You know, there are buckets of reasons why something is not your fault, not to mention the gazillion ways to avoid taking the blame (or doing anything to fix it). We are a nation which doesn't stop at passing the buck; we dodge it entirely. So with that in mind, and with a firm resolve not to do any more than I absolutely have to, I offer this book so people have an excuse not to think up their own excuses to get themselves out of a jam.

p.s. I would have written this book last year, but my printer cartridge ran out, my computer was down, my bunny rabbit chewed the cable and my parakeet's singing gave me a migrane headache!

I THOUGHT THAT THE WHOLE CREDIT LIMIT THING WAS A CHALLENGE TO SEE IF I CAN SPEND THAT MUCH MONEY. I CAN.

"I Didn't Do It!"

I HAVEN'T VISITED BECAUSE
ABSENCE MAKES THE
HEART GROW FONDER,
AND I WANT TO BE REALLY
GLAD TO SEE YOU.

"I Didn't Do It!"

MY BUTT ISN'T GETTING WIDER.
IT SIMPLY NEEDS TO HAVE IT'S
HORIZONTAL HOLD ADJUSTED.

7

I Didn't Do It!"

"I Didn't Do It!"

"I Didn't Do It!"

"I Didn't Do It!"

"I Didn't Do It!"

8

*I CAN'T PAY FOR LUNCH.
I'VE JUST RETURNED FROM
EUROPE AND ALL I HAVE IS LIRA.*

THE LIGHT WAS RED?
BUT I'M COLOR BLIND, OFFICER.

I Didn't Do It!"

"I Didn't Do It!"

"I Didn't Do It!"

"I Didn't Do It!"

"I Didn't Do It!"

9

"I Didn't Do It!"

Why haven't I written?
I didn't know
you could read.

10

"I Didn't Do It!"

I THOUGHT THE "E" ON MY GAS
GAUGE MEANT "ENOUGH".

You're not going bald.
You're shedding your
winter fur.

12

WHY SHOULD I SPEND TIME ON HAIR AND MAKE UP? I DON'T NEED TO BE BEAUTIFUL BECAUSE I'M BRILLIANT.

13

14

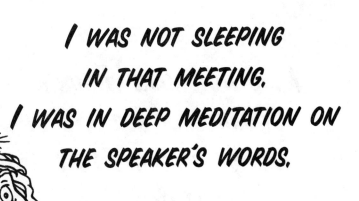

15

"I Didn't Do It!"

I DID NOT MAKE A MISTAKE,
I PURPOSELY SCREWED UP
AS AN OFFERING TO THE
GODS OF CHAOS.

16

"I Didn't Do It!"

I'M NOT LATE. I'M JUST
EXPERIMENTING WITH THE
FABRIC OF TIME.

17

"I Didn't Do It!"

"I Didn't Do It!"

"I Didn't Do It!"

"I Didn't Do It!"

"I Didn't Do It!"

18

HE'S NOT RUDE. HE JUST HAS A VERY LOW READING ON THE SOCIAL SKILLS SCALE.

I'M NOT GROUCHY. I'M JUST "HAPPINESS CHALLENGED".

I Didn't Do It!"

"I Didn't Do It!"

"I Didn't Do It!"

"I Didn't Do It!"

"I Didn't Do It!"

19

"I Didn't Do It!"

DIDN'T YOU GET MY FAX?

"I Didn't Do It!"

YOU DIDN'T GET A THANK YOU NOTE FROM ME BECAUSE I DON'T BELIEVE IN THE SENSELESS SLAUGHTER OF INNOCENT TREES FOR PERSONAL GRATIFICATION.

21

I CAN'T POSSIBLY
GO OUT WITH YOU.
I'M DREADFULLY ALLERGIC
TO BORING.

I DIDN'T FORGET MY GLASSES.
I LEFT THEM BEHIND
FOR POSTERITY.

23

24

"I Didn't Do It!"

SHE'S NOT GETTING OLD,
SHE'S JUST NEARING
HER EXPIRATION DATE.

"I Didn't Do It!"

BUT IF I CLEAN MY FRIDGE,
I'LL DESTROY AN
ENTIRE ECOSYSTEM.

I Didn't Do It!"

"I Didn't Do It!"

"I Didn't Do It!"

"I Didn't Do It!"

"I Didn't Do It!"

28

ARE YOU SURE YOU DON'T WANT TO KEEP HOLDING? YOU ARE ONLY 3 MINUTES AWAY FROM THE RECORD, YOU KNOW.

OF COURSE I WENT SHOPPING. I'M TRYING TO HELP STIMULATE THE NATION'S ECONOMY.

I Didn't Do It!"

"I Didn't Do It!"

"I Didn't Do It!"

"I Didn't Do It!"

"I Didn't Do It!"

29

"I Didn't Do It!"

WHY SHOULD I PAY MY POWER BILL?
I'D JUST BE SUBSIDIZING
ANOTHER HUGE CAPITALISTIC
CORPORATION WHICH OPPRESSES
THE DOWNTRODDEN WORKERS.

"I Didn't Do It!"

NO, I CAN'T WORK LATE.
MY GERBIL IS HAVING BABIES,
AND I'M HER LABOR COACH.

I'M NOT DETAIL ORIENTED. I FOCUS ON THE BIGGER PICTURE.

32

BUT HONEY, THAT WASN'T ANOTHER WOMAN I WAS HAVING LUNCH WITH. ONE OF MY FRIENDS IS A TRANSVESTITE, AND I WAS HELPING HIM NORMALIZE HIS FEELINGS.

33

WASH MY HANDS BEFORE I EAT? BUT I'LL BE USING A FORK, SO I'LL NEVER ACTUALLY TOUCH THE FOOD.

I HAD TO EAT 2 HELPINGS.
IN SOME CULTURES,
TURNING DOWN FOOD IS A
HORRIBLE INSULT.

"I Didn't Do It!"

I DON'T THINK OF IT AS
"STEALING YOUR PEN,"
I THINK OF IT AS
"COLLECTING MEMENTOS,"

"I Didn't Do It!"

BUT BY CRASHING INTO YOUR CAR, I'VE GIVEN YOU THE OPPORTUNITY TO SEE HOW WELL YOUR INSURANCE COMPANY'S CLAIM DEPARTMENT WORKS.

37

I Didn't Do It!"

"I Didn't Do It!"

"I Didn't Do It!"

"I Didn't Do It!"

"I Didn't Do It!"

NO, I'M NOT "PIGGING OUT." I'M ASSIMILATING CALORIC DATA.

SOMEONE HAD TO DRINK ALL THAT BEER TO KEEP THOSE BIG CLYDESDALE HORSES WORKING.

I Didn't Do It!"

"I Didn't Do It!"

"I Didn't Do It!"

"I Didn't Do It!"

"I Didn't Do It!"

"I Didn't Do It!"

DON'T THINK OF IT AS
"SPACED OUT", THINK OF IT AS
"EXPLORING THE
FINAL FRONTIER."

"I Didn't Do It!"

HE'S NOT STUPID,
HE'S JUST DOING SOME
TRACK WORK FOR HIS
TRAIN OF THOUGHT.

A BLATANT LIE -
AN OBVIOUS EXERCISE
IN CREATIVE FABRICATION.

42

I CAN'T POSSIBLY JOIN YOU FOR DINNER. BEING AROUND YOU DAZZLES ME SO MUCH THAT I CAN'T SEE MY PLATE.

43

NO NEED TO WORK OUT TODAY, BECAUSE I'VE ALREADY "DODGED A BULLET", "BACKPEDALED", "DANCED AROUND THE ISSUES" AND "FALLEN DOWN ON THE JOB."

45

"I Didn't Do It!"

I MAKE SO MANY MISTAKES
SO MY BOSS
WILL LOOK SMARTER.

46

"I Didn't Do It!"

O.K., SO I'M LATE.
I'M ALSO VERY WELL RESTED.

I Didn't Do It!"

"I Didn't Do It!"

"I Didn't Do It!"

"I Didn't Do It!"

"I Didn't Do It!"

48

*THE CHECK DIDN'T BOUNCE.
IT JUST FELL DOWN WITHOUT
A CUSHION OF MONEY.*

I CAN'T TAKE THE TRASH OUT.
THERE WOULD BE NOTHING LEFT
IN THE HOUSE.

I Didn't Do It!"

"I Didn't Do It!"

"I Didn't Do It!"

"I Didn't Do It!"

"I Didn't Do It!"

"I Didn't Do It!"

If I wait to clean the oven, eventually the stuff in it will catch fire and burn itself out.

50

"I Didn't Do It!"

YOU HAVE TO DRINK BEER WHEN YOU TRAVEL. YOU GENERALLY CAN'T DRINK THE WATER.

WHY SHOULD I CLEAN UP
WHAT THE DOGS DEPOSIT
IN MY YARD?
THEY'LL JUST MAKE MORE.

52

No, I didn't do what I told you I was going to do. You'd think I was dependable and start taking me for granted.

53

54

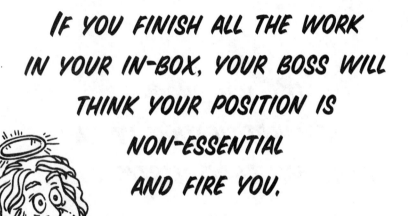

IF YOU FINISH ALL THE WORK IN YOUR IN-BOX, YOUR BOSS WILL THINK YOUR POSITION IS NON-ESSENTIAL AND FIRE YOU.

"I Didn't Do It!"

IT'S NOT SHOPPING,
IT'S PARTICIPATION IN THE
AMERICAN CAPITALISTIC IDEAL.

"I Didn't Do It!"

I WOULD CLEAN OUT
MY CLOSET, BUT NATURE
ABHORS A VACCUUM.

I Didn't Do It!"

"I Didn't Do It!"

"I Didn't Do It!"

"I Didn't Do It!"

"I Didn't Do It!"

58

HE'S LATE TO WORK BECAUSE HE WAS LIVING THE COMMUTE TO IT'S FULLEST.

"I Didn't Do It!"

"I Didn't Do It!"

"I Didn't Do It!"

"I Didn't Do It!"

"I Didn't Do It!"

BY NOT SHOVELING THE WALKS,
I AM ALLOWING NATURE
TO REMAIN UNDISTURBED.

59

"I Didn't Do It!"

*I WAS LOOKING
WHERE I WAS GOING.
I JUST WASN'T GOING
WHERE I WAS LOOKING.*

"I Didn't Do It!"

DRINKING?
OH, NO, OFFICER,
I WAS JUST CLEANING
MY TEETH WITH VODKA.

I WAS SLEEPING THROUGH THAT MEETING SO I WOULD BE WELL RESTED AND BE ABLE TO BOLT BACK TO MY WORK ENTHUSIASTICALLY.

62

RETURNING SOMETHING THAT SOMEONE GAVE YOU IS RUDE, SO NEVER RETURN PHONE CALLS.

63

CHANGE THE OIL IN THE CAR? BUT IT HASN'T USED UP ALL THE OIL I GAVE IT LAST TIME.

"I Didn't Do It!"

I HAVEN'T CLEANED OUT THE VEGETABLE
DRAWER IN THE REFRIGERATOR BECAUSE IF
I WAIT LONG ENOUGH, IT WILL MAKE A
COMPOST FOR THE GARDEN NEXT SPRING.

"I Didn't Do It!"

MY TURN TO CHANGE THE BABY?
BUT I'M HIS FATHER. I WAS ON THE
DESIGN TEAM. NOBODY TOLD ME I'D
BE ON THE MAINTENANCE TEAM, TOO.

I Didn't Do It!"

"I Didn't Do It!"

"I Didn't Do It!"

"I Didn't Do It!"

"I Didn't Do It!"

68

OUR LOVE IS SO FAR ABOVE THE "TRIVIAL GIFT STAGE" THAT I DIDN'T WANT TO INSULT YOU BY GIVING YOU AN ANNIVERSARY GIFT.

BUT WORKING ON THE HOUSE WOULD JUST INCREASE THE PROPERTY VALUE, AND WE'D HAVE TO PAY MORE TAXES.

I Didn't Do It!"

"I Didn't Do It!"

"I Didn't Do It!"

"I Didn't Do It!"

"I Didn't Do It!"

69

"I Didn't Do It!"

I'M NOT LOAFING,
I'M REGULATING MY
ENERGY OUTPUT.

"I Didn't Do It!"

MY ANSWERING MACHINE
ISN'T WORKING RIGHT.
IT KEEPS TAKING MESSAGES
FROM PEOPLE I DON'T
WANT TO TALK TO.

WATER THE GRASS.
CUT THE GRASS.
IT'S A VICIOUS CIRCLE.

I KNOW THE ANSWER,
BUT IT'S BEEN CLASSIFIED AS
"NEED TO KNOW", AND YOU
DON'T REALLY NEED TO KNOW.

73

I HAD TO GET DRUNK AND STUPID AT THE OFFICE PARTY SO THAT THERE WOULD BE SOME NEW OFFICE GOSSIP.

"I Didn't Do It!"

YES, I'M PAYING ATTENTION.
IT'S JUST THAT I'M DISTRACTED
BY THE BRILLIANCE OF
YOUR ORATORY, BOSS.

"I Didn't Do It!"

AGE - IT'S NOT THE YEARS,
IT'S THE DISTANCE COVERED.

"I Didn't Do It!"

"I Didn't Do It!"

"I Didn't Do It!"

"I Didn't Do It!"

"I Didn't Do It!"

BUT MOM, IF I PRACTICE MY _____ (insert the musical instrument of your choice) , **I'LL GET SO GOOD THAT I'LL END UP IN A BAND AND LIVE THE "SEX, DRUGS AND ROCK 'N' ROLL LIFESTYLE" OF A ROCK-STAR INSTEAD OF ATTENDING COLLEGE, GETTING A GOOD JOB AND RAISING WELL-ADJUSTED CHILDREN.**

BUT IF I DON'T BUY EXPENSIVE CLOTHES, ALL YOUR FRIENDS WILL THINK THAT I DON'T HAVE ANY CLASS.

I Didn't Do It!"

"I Didn't Do It!"

"I Didn't Do It!"

"I Didn't Do It!"

"I Didn't Do It!"

79

"I Didn't Do It!"

I DON'T HAVE ANY MONEY.
I'VE NEVER HAD ANY MONEY.
I NEVER WILL HAVE ANY MONEY.
AT LEAST I'M CONSISTENT.

"I Didn't Do It!"

SINCE YOU COOKED THE MEAL,
YOU FEEL YOU SHOULDN'T HAVE TO
DO DISHES. BUT DON'T YOU WANT
TO FINISH WHAT YOU STARTED?

81

LET'S TAKE TURNS HERE.
YOU COOK; I'LL EAT;
YOU DO DISHES.

It's not a good idea to buy something from door to door salesmen. It will just encourage them.

83

I CAN'T SLEEP OVER THE LONELY SOBBING OF THAT LEFTOVER CHOCOLATE CAKE. I'D BETTER GO COMFORT IT.

I KNOW IT'S NOT YOUR FAULT. BUT THE PERSON WHOSE FAULT IT IS ISN'T HERE, AND I WANT TO YELL AT SOMEONE NOW.

"I Didn't Do It!"

I HAVE TO CHECK WITH
MY SPOUSE. FIRST, I HAVE TO
GET A SPOUSE, AND THEN
I'LL HAVE TO CHECK WITH HIM.

"I Didn't Do It!"

I DON'T THINK OF IT AS
A REFRIGERATOR RAID.
IT'S MORE LIKE
"INVENTORY CONTROL".

I Didn't Do It!"

"I Didn't Do It!"

"I Didn't Do It!"

"I Didn't Do It!"

"I Didn't Do It!"

MY KID BROTHER DID IT.

WHY EAT HEALTHY NOW?
I'VE ALREADY TRASHED MY BODY.

"I Didn't Do It!"

"I Didn't Do It!"

"I Didn't Do It!"

"I Didn't Do It!"

"I Didn't Do It!"

89

"I Didn't Do It!"

I CAN EAT THOSE DONUTS IF I DON'T EAT LUNCH. ALL WEEK.

"I Didn't Do It!"

I'M NOT AS CREATIVE AS YOU ARE.
I DON'T HAVE ACCESS
TO THE SAME MEDICATIONS.

IT'S A LANGUAGE PROBLEM.
HE DOESN'T USE ANY.

I DIDN'T SPEND TOO MUCH MONEY.
I JUST DIDN'T EARN
AS MUCH AS I SPENT.

93

BY PULLING OUT IN FRONT OF YOU, I'M ALLOWING YOU TO TEST YOUR ANTI-LOCK BRAKING SYSTEM.

95

"I Didn't Do It!"

WEED THE GARDEN?
BUT AREN'T WEEDS
LIVING CREATURES, TOO?

96

"I Didn't Do It!"

IT'S NOT REALLY GAMBLING.
IT'S AN EXPERIMENT
IN THE LAWS OF AVERAGES.

I Didn't Do It!"

"I Didn't Do It!"

"I Didn't Do It!"

"I Didn't Do It!"

"I Didn't Do It!"

98

*I GOT YOUR MESSAGE,
BUT I COULDN'T READ
MY SECRETARY'S HANDWRITING.*

I THOUGHT THE "E" ON MY GAS GAUGE MEANT "EXTRA".

I Didn't Do It!"

"I Didn't Do It!"

"I Didn't Do It!"

"I Didn't Do It!"

"I Didn't Do It!"

99

WE'D LOVE TO HAVE YOU VISIT.
BUT WE'RE UNDER
STRICT QUARANTINE.

100

"I Didn't Do It!"

I TRIED TO DRESS UP FOR WORK. BUT MY STOCKINGS WERE RUNNING FASTER THAN I WAS.

I'M CALLING IN SICK TODAY.
I'VE GOT BOOGIE FEVER.

BUT I DO LOVE YOU.
I JUST LOVE
FOOTBALL MORE.

105

"I Didn't Do It!"

NO, WE CAN'T HAVE A DISCUSSION ABOUT OUR RELATIONSHIP. I SPENT SO MUCH TIME TELLING MY CO-WORKERS HOW WONDERFUL YOU ARE THAT MY TONGUE IS TIRED.

"I Didn't Do It!"

IT WOULD BE UNFAIR IF I HAVE TO WALK
THE DOG. SEE, THE DOG HAS **4** LEGS AND
I ONLY HAVE **2**. I'D HAVE TO WORK
TWICE AS HARD AS THE DOG.

I Didn't Do It!"

"I Didn't Do It!"

"I Didn't Do It!"

"I Didn't Do It!"

"I Didn't Do It!"

108

WELL, I HAD TO EAT ALL THAT DESSERT AFTER DINNER. IT WILL BE 12 HOURS BEFORE I CAN EAT AGAIN.

I WAS PLAYING COMPUTER GAMES TO TEST THE PROCESSING SPEED OF THE MACHINE.

"I Didn't Do It!"

"I Didn't Do It!"

"I Didn't Do It!"

"I Didn't Do It!"

"I Didn't Do It!"

109

"I Didn't Do It!"

THAT PROJECT ISN'T FINISHED YET
BECAUSE I'M STILL IN THE
PLANNING PHASE. I'M PLANNING
TO DO IT LATER.

"I Didn't Do It!"

I WASN'T WRONG,
I WAS JUST
"CORRECTNESS CHALLENGED".

111

No, we're not lost.
We're just exploring
alternate routes to
our destination.

CAN'T COME TO WORK TODAY.
I'M PAYING OFF A HEAVY
COSMIC DEBT INCURRED
IN A PAST LIFE.

113

I FAILED THE EXAM ON PURPOSE. I'M TRYING TO THROW OFF THE CURVE.

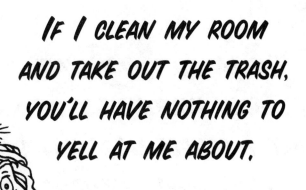

If I clean my room and take out the trash, you'll have nothing to yell at me about.

115

"I Didn't Do It!"

THE LAUNDRY CAN WAIT.
IT'S BEEN WAITING ALL WEEK,
AND A COUPLE MORE HOURS
WON'T HURT ANYTHING.

No, you're not boring me.
It's those cold pills I took.

I Didn't Do It!"

"I Didn't Do It!"

"I Didn't Do It!"

"I Didn't Do It!"

"I Didn't Do It!"

118

I CAN'T WORK OUT TODAY. I REALLY DON'T LOOK GOOD IN THOSE STRETCHY LITTLE PANTS.

IF I DON'T GO FISHING THIS WEEKEND, THE FISH WILL OVERPOPULATE THE LAKE, AND AN ENTIRE AQUATIC ECOSYSTEM WILL SUFFER.

I Didn't Do It!"

"I Didn't Do It!"

"I Didn't Do It!"

"I Didn't Do It!"

"I Didn't Do It!"

119

"I Didn't Do It!"

*I HAVE TO GO SHOPPING AGAIN,
OTHERWISE OUR MONEY
WILL PILE UP AND WE'LL
HAVE TO PAY MORE TAXES.*

"I Didn't Do It!"

BUY MORE POWER TOOLS.
SOMEDAY OUR CIVILIZATION
WILL COLLAPSE AND ONLY THOSE
WITH LOTS OF POWER TOOLS
WILL BE ABLE TO REBUILD.

WON'T BE IN TOMORROW.
HAVE TO TAKE MY
MOTHER-IN-LAW TO THE VET.

122

LEAVING EARLY TODAY, BOSS. I'M HAVING MY BROOM REBRISTLED.

123

TAKING A LONG LUNCH TODAY, BOSS. MY SPOUSE AND I ARE GOING TO BE ON A TALK SHOW ABOUT "COMPLETE LOSERS AND THE PEOPLE WHO MARRY THEM."

MY PAST LIFE EXPERIENCE IS INTRUDING ON MY PRESENT LIFE. I KEEP THINKING I'M A 15TH CENTURY SCOTTISH WARRIOR.

"I Didn't Do It!"

PLEASE EXCUSE JUNIOR
FOR BEING ABSENT YESTERDAY.
IT TOOK SOME TIME TO RAISE BAIL.

"I Didn't Do It!"

WE'VE GOT A BRAND NEW, HIGH-POWERED, STATE-OF-THE-ART COMPUTER. NOW WE CAN REALLY SCREW THINGS UP.

"I Didn't Do It!"

"I Didn't Do It!"

"I Didn't Do It!"

"I Didn't Do It!"

"I Didn't Do It!"

128

OUR PHONE SYSTEM IS SO NEW AND IMPROVED THAT IT COMES WITH A "HOLD" BUTTON AND A "FORGET" BUTTON. I PUSHED THE WRONG ONE.

THAT DECISION MUST BE MADE BY A COMMITTEE. DON'T HOLD YOUR BREATH.

I Didn't Do It!"

"I Didn't Do It!"

"I Didn't Do It!"

"I Didn't Do It!"

"I Didn't Do It!"

129

"I Didn't Do It!"

THE SYSTEM IS DOWN
AND WE'RE FRESH OUT
OF ANTI-DEPRESSANTS.

"I Didn't Do It!"

DON'T YOU HAVE E-MAIL?
I DON'T EVEN OWN A
PENCIL AND PAPER ANYMORE.

I'M NOT CHEAP,
I HAPPEN TO BELIEVE
THAT "KITSCH" IS TRENDY.

132

*I NEED TO EAT 2 SERVINGS.
IT'S PRETTY BAD STUFF
AND HEAVEN ONLY KNOWS
WHAT IT WOULD DO TO AN
UNTRAINED STOMACH.*

133

BUT IF WE GO OUT TONIGHT WE'LL JUST BURN FOSSIL FUELS AND POLLUTE OUR ALREADY DAMAGED ECOSYSTEM.

YOU'RE SO PRETTY,
YOU DON'T NEED DIAMONDS.

135

"I Didn't Do It!"

WE DON'T NEED A VACATION.
ANYTIME WE'RE TOGETHER
IT'S PARADISE.

"I Didn't
Do It!"

WE'D LOVE TO SEE YOU.
FAX US A PICTURE.

I Didn't Do It!"

"I Didn't Do It!"

"I Didn't Do It!"

"I Didn't Do It!"

"I Didn't Do It!"

138

CLEAN UP?
BUT THE GRUNGE LOOK
IS SO IN.

I'LL START MY DIET TOMORROW. TODAY I'M STILL IN THE "WEIGHTING" PERIOD.

I Didn't Do It!"

"I Didn't Do It!"

"I Didn't Do It!"

"I Didn't Do It!"

"I Didn't Do It!"

139

"I Didn't Do It!"

IF I SHOVEL THE WALKS NOW,
I'LL THROW MY BACK OUT AND
HAVE TO TAKE 3 DAYS OFF TO HEAL.

"I Didn't Do It!"

IT WAS A PHYSICS ERROR.
MY CAR AND HIS CAR WERE
ATTEMPTING TO SIMULTANEOUSLY
OCCUPY THE SAME SPACE.

It's not a bad report card.
It's a wide open road
to improvement.

142

NEW CLOTHES
KEEP AMERICAN TEXTILE
WORKERS EMPLOYED.

143

THE CHECK IS LATE,
BECAUSE I KNOW HOW MUCH
YOU LOVE SUSPENSE.

144

I WASN'T GOOFING AROUND.
I WAS SPONTANEOUSLY RELAXING.

145

"I Didn't Do It!"

I'M NOT GAINING WEIGHT,
I'M LOSING SLIM.

"I Didn't Do It!"

THE COPIER IS DOWN, THE FAX IS OUT OF PAPER AND THE HARD DISK IN THE COMPUTER IS TOASTED. WE'RE EXPERIENCING TECHNICAL DIFFICULTIES.

I Didn't Do It!"

"I Didn't Do It!"

"I Didn't Do It!"

"I Didn't Do It!"

"I Didn't Do It!"

148

YOUR BIRTHDAY?
BUT YOU'RE TIMELESS.

I Didn't Do It!"

"I Didn't Do It!"

I'M NOT GROUCHY.
I'M SUB-PERKY.

"I Didn't Do It!"

"I Didn't Do It!"

"I Didn't Do It!"

"I Didn't Do It!"

I DON'T WANT TO GO TO WORK. IF I AMASS TOO MUCH WEALTH, I'LL BECOME A RICH SNOB AND ALL MY FRIENDS WILL HATE ME.

"I Didn't Do It!"

I'M TERMINALLY ILL.
I'M SICK OF
MY COMPUTER.

151

I'M NOT UNEMPLOYED.
I'M JUST UNWILLING
TO COMMIT TO A JOB.

152

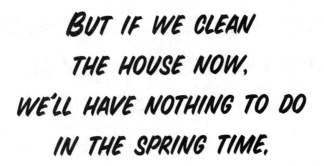

*BUT IF WE CLEAN
THE HOUSE NOW,
WE'LL HAVE NOTHING TO DO
IN THE SPRING TIME.*

153

I MISSED MY TURN THIS MORNING, AND THE FIRST CHANCE I GOT TO TURN THE CAR AROUND WAS IN LAS VEGAS.

155

"I Didn't Do It!"

I'M NOT BROKE.
I JUST HAVE AN UNEVEN
BILLS-TO-MONEY RATIO.

"I Didn't Do It!"

BY ONLY SHOWING UP OCCASIONALLY FOR WORK, I'M AVOIDING CAREER BURN OUT.

157

I Didn't Do It!"

"I Didn't Do It!"

"I Didn't Do It!"

"I Didn't Do It!"

"I Didn't Do It!"

158

I'M NOT GOOFING OFF, I'M JUST TAKING SEVERAL BREAKS IN A ROW.

IT'S SUCH A SHOCK TO GO BACK TO WORK AFTER A VACATION. SHOCKS ARE BAD FOR YOUR SYSTEM. MAYBE YOU SHOULD JUST EXTEND YOUR VACATION.

I Didn't Do It!"

"I Didn't Do It!"

"I Didn't Do It!"

"I Didn't Do It!"

"I Didn't Do It!"

159

"I Didn't Do It!"

I HAVE TO SAMPLE
THOSE COOKIES TO MAKE
SURE THEY'RE ALL RIGHT
FOR MY FAMILY.

"I Didn't Do It!"

WE HAVEN'T LOST
THAT LOVING FEELING.
WE'VE BORED IT TO DEATH.

IT'S NOT THAT I DON'T KNOW,
IT'S THAT I DON'T CARE.

NO, WE'RE NOT GOING TO HAVE KIDS. WE DON'T WANT TO SHARE OUR TOYS.

163

I'M NOT DRUNK. I'M IN A PRE-HANGOVER CONDITION.

164

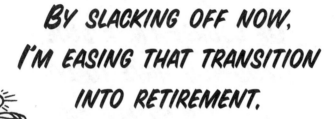

165

"I Didn't Do It!"

OF COURSE I'M A SLOB,
AND YOU HAVE TO DO
EVERYTHING FOR ME.
CALL IT JOB SECURITY.

"I Didn't Do It!"

I NEVER GOT A BILL!
(OF COURSE, I MOVED
3 TIMES AND HAVE BEGUN
USING AN ALIAS...)

167

Other Titles by Great Quotations

201 Best Things Ever Said
The ABC's of Parenting
African-American Wisdom
As A Cat Thinketh
Astrology for Cats
The Be-Attitudes
The Best of Friends
The Birthday Astrologer
Chicken Soup
Chocoholic Reasonettes
The Cornerstones of Success
Daddy & Me
Fantastic Father,
   Dependable Dad
For Mother, A Bouquet
   of Sentiments
Global Wisdom
Golden Years, Golden Words
Grandma, I Love You
Growing Up in Toyland
Happiness Is Found Along
   the Way
High Anxieties
Hollywords

Hooked on Golf
I Didn't Do It
Ignorance is Bliss
In Celebration of Women
Inspirations
Interior Design for Idiots
I'm Not Over the Hill
The Lemonade Handbook
Let's Talk Decorating
Life's Lessons
Life's Simple Pleasures
A Lifetime of Love
A Light Heart Lives Long
Midwest Wisdom
Mommy & Me
Mrs. Aesop's Fables
Mother, I Love You
Motivating Quotes
   for Motivated People
Mrs. Murphy's Laws
Mrs. Webster's Dictionary
My Daughter,
   My Special Friend
Only a Sister

The Other Species
Parenting 101
The Perfect Man
Reflections
Romantic Rhapsody
The Rose Mystique
The Secret Language of Men
The Secret Language
   of Women
The Secrets in Your Face
The Secrets in Your Name
Social Disgraces
Some Things Never Change
The Sports Page
Sports Widow
Stress or Sanity
A Teacher Is Better Than
   Two Books
TeenAge of Insanity
Thanks from the Heart
Things You'll Learn...
Wedding Wonders
Words From the Coach
Working Woman's World

GREAT QUOTATIONS PUBLISHING COMPANY
Glendale Heights, IL 60139
Phone (630) 582-2800 • Fax (630) 582-2813